I dedicate this book to the unwavering pillars of my life—my sons and my wife. Your steadfast belief in me, unyielding support, and the freedom to be the protector our family needs have been the driving force behind every chapter of this work.

In the face of uncertainties, your trust has fueled my commitment to ensuring our family's safety and well-being. This dedication is a testament to the love, strength, and unity that bind us together.

May the lessons within these pages stand as a testament to the profound influence you've had on my journey. Your belief in me has been the bedrock on which I've built not only this book but also the foundation of our family's resilience.

Thank you for being the constant force that propels me forward and for allowing me to be the person I need to be—the protector, the provider, and the guide through the unknown. This book is a tribute to our shared journey and a token of my profound gratitude.

With love and dedication,

Dear Reader,

Congratulations on acquiring this invaluable guide to survival and preparedness. In a world where uncertainties abound, your decision to delve into this book demonstrates foresight and a commitment to safeguarding yourself and your loved ones.

In the pages that follow, you will find a comprehensive exploration of survival skills, emergency communications, effective action planning, and the essential mindset needed to navigate unforeseen challenges. This book is not merely a collection of strategies; it is a roadmap to equip you with the knowledge to thrive in the face of adversity.

Enter the tactical realm of survival with an expert boasting over two decades of active-duty military experience, combat tours in Iraq, and anti-human trafficking operations in South America. Post-military, the author honed advanced medical skills as an emergency medical technician in California, transitioning seamlessly into active law enforcement in Washington state.

This book is a strategic blueprint, forged in the crucible of real-world scenarios, offering battle-tested insights. Dive into the rules of survival, master effective communication amid chaos, execute discreet urban navigation, and foster a battle-ready mindset. Strike the perfect equilibrium between preparedness and normalcy, ensuring you and your loved ones are not just survivors but masters of the unforeseen.

But this book is more than just information—it's a guide to personal transformation. The benefits extend beyond the theoretical; they translate into tangible preparedness, enhancing your ability to face challenges head-on.

So, without further ado, I invite you to dive into the chapters ahead, absorb the wisdom, and begin your path to a more secure future. Arm yourself with the knowledge to thrive amidst uncertainties, and let this book be your guide to mastering the art of survival.

Your journey starts now.

Contents

Chapter 1: The Foundation of Survival

In a world marred by crisis, civil unrest, and constant uncertainty, the need for survival skills is paramount. The cornerstone of survival lies in understanding the rules of three – the three minutes without air, three days without water, and three weeks without food. In this chaos, preparation becomes not just a choice but a necessity.

Understanding the simplicity of the rules of three guides us through prioritization. While stockpiling is crucial, the importance of dry stores such as salt, sugar, flour, and baking soda cannot be overstated. These items, with their secondary uses, prove invaluable in times of crisis. Consider the historical role of sugar in making IVs during the Civil War, showcasing the adaptability of basic supplies.

Moreover, survival transcends merely storing resources; it entails the ability to generate them. A seed vault becomes a vital asset, as agricultural skills prove indispensable for the long term. Knowing the local fauna, understanding vegetation, and recognizing weather patterns become essential components of this skill set.

Water, a fundamental element for survival, deserves meticulous attention. The human body's composition underscores its significance, and calculating daily water needs becomes crucial. Storing water, considering its chemical properties for sanitation, and mastering water filtration techniques emerge as key survival skills.

Yet, even the most seasoned preppers sometimes overlook the critical importance of respiratory protection. Three minutes without air renders other preparations futile. Thus, prioritizing proper respiratory gear becomes the foremost goal in the hierarchy of survival needs.

In summary, survival in a world fraught with crisis demands a holistic approach. The rules of three serve as a compass, guiding us through the essentials: air, water, and food. Preparation involves not just accumulating resources but understanding their versatility. In this volatile world, adaptability and a multifaceted skill set are the true keys to survival.

Chapter 2: Navigating the Airwaves: Communication in the Abyss

In the tumult of a chaotic crisis, the thread that binds survival often rests in effective communication. This chapter delves into the intricacies of emergency communication, exploring electronic means, addressing potential vulnerabilities, and unveiling ingenious methods to safeguard sensitive information amid uncertainty.

Electronic Communication: A Double-Edged Sword

Citizens Band (CB) Radio
Citizens Band radios emerge as a reliable tool for short-distance communication. Their simplicity and widespread availability make them an accessible choice. However, limited range and susceptibility to interference pose inherent challenges.

Ham Radio (Amateur Radio)
Stepping up the communication hierarchy, Ham radios offer extended ranges and more versatile frequencies. Yet, the need for licensing and technical expertise could prove a barrier for many. Nevertheless, they stand as robust tools for organized and secure communication.

GMRS (General Mobile Radio Service)
GMRS devices bridge the gap, providing longer ranges without the complexity of Ham radios. Licensing requirements and potential for misuse, however, pose considerations in their adoption.

The Cybersecurity Conundrum

In an era where cyber threats loom large, the reliance on electronic communication introduces vulnerabilities. A crisis might render existing infrastructure nonexistent, making electronic communication even more critical. A cyber attack could disrupt or compromise these channels, emphasizing the need for contingency plans.

Encrypting the Unseen: The Art of Securing Communications

When the enemy's ears may be tuning into your frequency, encrypting messages becomes paramount. Without access to established encryption methods, creating your own cryptographic system could be a clandestine necessity. Developing a personalized alphabet and deciphering methods becomes a strategic approach, ensuring your vital information remains a mystery to potential adversaries.

The Silent Language: Visual Communication

In the chaos of a major disaster or civil unrest, visual communication assumes an underrated yet pivotal role. Understanding hand gestures within a group becomes a silent language, offering a means of conveying essential information without compromising operational security. This non-verbal communication could mean the difference between cohesion and chaos.

Data Gathering for Informed Decisions

Electronic communication transcends mere chatter; it becomes a tool for gathering data and assembling a comprehensive battle picture. Amid the chaos, collecting information over time allows survivors to make informed decisions – whether to hunker down or mobilize. The ability to share real-time information expands the collective awareness, a crucial asset in navigating the unknown.

The Tapestry of Survival: Weaving Communication into Resilience

In summary, effective communication in times of crisis is the golden thread weaving through the fabric of survival. The nuances of various electronic communication tools, coupled with the ever-present cybersecurity challenge, require survivors to adapt, innovate, and encrypt. Visual communication adds a layer of subtlety to group dynamics, while data gathering becomes the linchpin for informed decision-making. As we navigate the abyss of uncertainty, communication emerges not just as a means of survival but as a strategic imperative in the relentless pursuit of resilience.

Chapter 3: Crafting a Resilient Emergency Action Plan

In the unpredictable landscape of civil unrest and emergencies, the foundation of survival lies in a meticulously crafted emergency action plan. This chapter explores the intricate aspects of building a robust plan, from curating a trustworthy social circle to assembling a skilled and reliable team.

Pruning the Social Circle: The Importance of Trust

The peace-time principle of keeping your social circle small assumes paramount importance in times of crisis. Those invited into your emergency action plan must be individuals whose trustworthiness has been established during calmer periods. This foresight ensures that when chaos descends, the cohesion and reliability of your group remain intact.

Testing the Trust: Crucial Assessments

Building trust is a gradual process, and certain assessments can provide insights into the reliability of potential team members. Initiating discussions on hypothetical emergency scenarios gauges their preparedness mindset. Conducting small, low-stakes tasks together assesses teamwork and reliability. Observing how individuals respond to stress or adversity serves as a litmus test for their suitability in high-pressure situations.

Building a Team: Complementary Skills and Roles

A successful emergency action plan hinges on the strength and diversity of the team. Each member should not only understand their responsibilities but also bring a unique skill set to the table. A mechanic ensures that vehicles and equipment remain operational. Someone with a background in communications guarantees that the flow of information remains intact. Security and law enforcement expertise contribute to the group's safety, while military veterans offer insights into tactical organization.

Off-Grid Survival: The Importance of Varied Skills

Civil unrest may necessitate an off-grid existence, requiring the team to be self-sufficient for extended periods. Skills in agriculture become invaluable, making a gardener a vital asset. Each member must be able to contribute to the collective survival effort, from growing food to maintaining security. The ability to function independently while contributing to the group's well-being underscores the strength of the team.

Operational Security: Trust in Times of Crisis

Welcoming individuals into your emergency action plan demands meticulous consideration. Evaluating whether potential team members might bring additional family members necessitates a deeper level of trust. Operational security becomes paramount, and testing trustworthiness extends beyond the individual to encompass their immediate connections. Trust, once broken, could jeopardize the entire group, emphasizing the importance of discretion.

Revealing the Plan: Timing is Trust

The revelation of the full action plan should coincide with the establishment of unwavering trust among group members. Detailing movement plans, security protocols, and strategic locations prematurely risks compromising the entire endeavor. Each member must prove their commitment and reliability before the collective strategy is unveiled.

In conclusion, the construction of an effective emergency action plan requires meticulous planning and a discerning eye for trustworthiness. From the deliberate selection of a trustworthy social circle to the careful assembly of a skilled and diverse team, every facet plays a crucial role. As trust is tested and proven, the detailed plan gradually unfolds, providing a solid foundation for survival in times of crisis.

Chapter 4: Operationalizing Your Emergency Action Plan

Creating a comprehensive emergency action plan is just the first step in fortifying your survival strategy. The true efficacy of the plan is realized through rigorous practice, consideration of various threats, and strategic utilization of equipment. This chapter explores the critical aspects of bringing your emergency action plan to life, ensuring seamless execution in times of crisis.

From Paper to Practice: The Crucial Step

A plan on paper remains theoretical until it undergoes the crucible of practice. Understanding distances, potential threats, and estimating travel times to the safe location become pivotal. The team must rehearse the planned movements, identifying angles against possible pursuers and mastering the art of navigation without reliance on electronic devices.

Essential Equipment: Navigational Tools

As the team embarks on practice sessions, the necessity of basic equipment becomes evident. Paper maps and compasses emerge as indispensable tools, offering a fail-safe alternative to electronic navigation. Understanding how to read terrain, identify landmarks, and choose optimal routes without relying on technology is a fundamental skill.

Securing the Digital Trail: Electronic Sanitization

Electronic devices, while invaluable, can become liabilities in the wrong hands. Ensuring that each team member sanitizes themselves electronically before reaching the safe location becomes paramount. The digital footprint left by phones and bank cards can be exploited, highlighting the need for a covert approach in the face of cyber warfare.

Secondary Location: A Strategic Imperative

In a world marred by civil unrest or potential government takeover, a secondary location takes on heightened importance. The act of sanitizing oneself must extend beyond the primary safe location. A secondary rendezvous point ensures that individuals cannot be electronically tracked to their ultimate destination, providing an added layer of security.

Ghosting the Electronic Trail: A Necessity

To achieve true operational security, team members must shed any remnants of their former electronic selves. Becoming a ghost, devoid of electronic detection, is not just a precaution; it becomes a survival imperative. This includes abandoning the use of newer vehicles laden with trackable technology and making decisions within the emergency action plan that prioritize stealth and evasion.

The Transformation: From Plan to Reality

In conclusion, the transformation of an emergency action plan from concept to reality hinges on meticulous practice and strategic considerations. The team must become adept at executing movements, understanding threats, and adapting to unforeseen circumstances. Navigational tools and electronic sanitization serve as critical components, while the establishment of a secondary location and the embrace of electronic ghosting elevate the plan to a level of sophistication necessary for navigating the tumultuous waters of civil unrest and potential anarchy.

Chapter 5: The Crucial Survival Skills: A Holistic Approach

In the dynamic landscape of potential civil unrest and emergencies, acquiring a diverse set of survival skills is not just advisable – it's essential. This chapter delves into the multifaceted skills and experiences you should be cultivating now to ensure the well-being and resilience of yourself and your loved ones.

Medical Proficiency: The First Line of Defense

Gaining proficiency in medical skills is paramount, especially when access to conventional healthcare facilities may be compromised. Basic and advanced medical training, encompassing patient assessments, vital sign monitoring, wound closure, and infection prevention, forms the bedrock of your ability to treat injuries and illnesses within your family. Understanding anatomy becomes a prerequisite for effective care, ensuring that you can respond promptly and appropriately in the absence of professional medical assistance.

Medication Management: Beyond the Basics

For individuals in your family requiring daily medication, securing a reliable supply during emergencies becomes a critical concern. Hospitals and pharmacies may become inaccessible or depleted, necessitating a proactive plan. Exploring holistic approaches to healthcare, such as cultivating medicinal plants, empowers you with the knowledge to maintain health without relying solely on pharmaceuticals.

Water Procurement and Management

The ability to purify, sanitize, filter, and store water is fundamental to survival. Acquiring skills in water management ensures a sustained supply, safeguarding against potential shortages or contamination. This expertise becomes especially crucial as traditional sources become unreliable or inaccessible during major disturbances.

Agricultural Proficiency: Nurturing Self-Sufficiency

In times of prolonged emergencies, dry stores may deplete or become compromised. Acquiring agricultural skills transforms you into a self-sufficient provider. Knowledge of planting, cultivating, and harvesting ensures a renewable source of food, offering sustainability beyond the limitations of stored provisions.

Self-Defense and Tactical Awareness

As societal norms fray during emergencies, self-defense skills become indispensable. Basic self-defense and tactical training equip you and your team to protect yourselves and your resources. This is not just about firearms; it's about understanding situational awareness, defensive strategies, and de-escalation techniques to navigate potential threats.

Firearm Safety and Competency

For those integrating firearms into their emergency action plan, firearm safety and competency are non-negotiable. Understanding how to handle, move, and utilize firearms safely maximizes your protection while minimizing risks. This skill set ensures the responsible and effective use of firearms as tools for defense.

Multilingual Communication: Bridging Divides

Effective communication extends beyond electronic devices. Learning a language relevant to potential emergency scenarios equips you with the ability to interact and collaborate with individuals who may not speak your native language. This skill fosters understanding, cooperation, and collective resilience across linguistic barriers.

In conclusion, a holistic approach to survival skills is the key to comprehensive preparedness. Medical proficiency, medication management, water procurement, agricultural skills, self-defense, firearm safety, and multilingual communication collectively form a robust foundation. Cultivating these skills today ensures that when the crucible of crisis descends, you possess the knowledge and capabilities to safeguard yourself and your loved ones with confidence and resilience.

Chapter 6: The Gray Man Tactics in Urban Movement

Surviving in an urban setting during times of crisis demands a strategic approach to movement – the Gray Man tactics. The philosophy is simple: avoid standing out and blend into your surroundings. In this chapter, we explore the nuances of the Gray Man tactics, emphasizing the art of subtle navigation and the imperative need to adapt to the herd mentality in urban settings.

The Essence of Gray Man Tactics

Ditch the military tactical gear and flashy equipment. The Gray Man does not draw attention but seamlessly blends in with the environment. The goal is to look less desirable, making it easier to move around without attracting unwanted attention.

Dressing the Part

Looking like a less desirable individual in an urban setting can be an advantage. Appearing dirty or possibly homeless decreases the likelihood of becoming a target. Flashy attire and expensive gear only make you conspicuous, inviting unnecessary risks.

Navigating Herd Mentality

Understanding and utilizing the herd mentality is crucial. If a group is moving together, find a way to blend in, leapfrog to another group, or navigate to a different area. Standing out in a collective movement increases vulnerability. The Gray Man adapts to the behaviors of the surroundings, enhancing the ability to move unnoticed.

Chameleon-like Adaptation

Being a chameleon means mirroring the actions of those around you. If the environment dictates a specific behavior, mimic it until you can move away discreetly. The Gray Man skill lies in seamlessly adapting to the prevailing circumstances without drawing attention.

Personal Safety and Decisive Actions

If you suspect you're being followed, the Gray Man must make decisive decisions. Choosing a checkpoint strategically, possibly appearing vulnerable, is a tactical move. A less desirable appearance and the element of surprise enhance the chances of safeguarding yourself in a challenging situation.

Traveling Light: The Urban Essential

In urban movement, traveling light is not just a suggestion – it's a necessity. Large bags and conspicuous items draw attention. The Gray Man knows how to move stealthily, carrying only what is absolutely essential to avoid becoming a target.

Sere Training: Military Wisdom

Sere training (Survival, Evasion, Resistance, and Escape) equips individuals with essential skills for urban survival. Learning about sere tactics enhances your ability to navigate through challenging situations, ensuring that you can adapt and overcome potential threats effectively.

The Element of Surprise

Being the Gray Man means employing the element of surprise when needed. Looking like an undesirable or someone who wouldn't put up a fight can catch potential threats off guard, providing a momentary advantage.

The Art of Blending: When in Rome

Adopting the "When in Rome" mindset involves acting like the locals. While this doesn't mean engaging in criminal behavior, it does require blending in with the crowd and adapting to the prevailing actions to move discreetly through urban settings.

In conclusion, the Gray Man tactics are an art form in urban survival. From dressing the part and navigating herd mentalities to adapting like a chameleon and making strategic decisions, each facet contributes to the mastery of moving unnoticed in an urban environment. The Gray Man embraces the shadows, seamlessly weaving through the chaos of crisis while prioritizing personal safety and survival.

Chapter 7: Forging the Survival Mindset: Clarity Amidst Chaos

In the crucible of major emergencies and societal collapse, the ability to maintain a strong survival mindset is the linchpin that separates those who endure from those who falter. This chapter delves into the intricacies of developing a resilient mindset, emphasizing key psychological aspects crucial for survival in life-or-death situations.

The Importance of Breath: Oxygen as a Lifeline

Amidst the chaos, it's crucial to remember the simplicity of breathing. Most individuals tend to freeze in the face of extreme survival situations, hindering proper gas exchange and clouding judgment. The foundation of any survival mindset begins with a conscious effort to breathe, ensuring oxygen flow for clear-headed decision-making.

Combating Tunnel Vision: A 360° Battle Picture

The instinct to focus on a single threat can be detrimental in an environment rife with potential dangers. Developing situational awareness becomes paramount. The ability to create a 360° battle picture, identify multiple threats, and strategically navigate towards the least resistant path empowers individuals to maneuver through crises with agility.

Action Over Analysis: Critical Thinking on the Move

Paralysis by analysis can be fatal. In the midst of emergencies, individuals often hesitate, questioning why and how the situation unfolded. The survival mindset requires an immediate shift from analysis to action. Critical thinking on the move is the key – making decisions swiftly based on training and experience to navigate through the chaos.

Acceptance in the Face of Adversity

Survival demands acceptance of the reality unfolding. When confronted with life-or-death situations, individuals must overcome the inclination to question and resist. Accepting the situation at hand, acknowledging threats, and understanding that one's primary responsibility is personal safety and that of their loved ones is crucial for effective decision-making.

Risk Versus Reward: Harsh Decisions for Survival

In the tumult of chaos, distinguishing between immediate threats and potential risks becomes imperative. The survival mindset involves making calculated and, at times, harsh decisions. Prioritizing personal safety and the safety of one's family over external circumstances requires an unwavering commitment to risk versus reward analysis.

Training the Mind for Survival

Cultivating a survival mindset is an ongoing process. Mental resilience is forged through training, exposure to stressors, and a commitment to mastering the psychological aspects of survival. Building mental toughness involves simulating crisis scenarios, practicing decision-making under pressure, and reinforcing the ability to remain focused and decisive.

Thriving Amidst Chaos

Survival is not just about enduring; it's about thriving. A well-honed survival mindset equips individuals to navigate through the chaos, make sound decisions, and emerge on the other side with resilience intact. Acceptance, action, and a calculated approach to risks contribute to a mindset that not only survives but thrives amidst the most challenging circumstances.

In conclusion, the survival mindset is the compass guiding individuals through the storm of emergencies. From the fundamental act of breathing to creating a 360° battle picture and making critical decisions on the move, each aspect contributes to mental resilience. Embracing the survival mindset ensures that, even in the face of chaos, individuals can navigate through the storm and emerge stronger on the other side.

Chapter 8: The Crucial Role of Physical Fitness in Survival

Survival extends beyond a mere mindset or the possession of survival gear; it is an intricate dance with the physical demands imposed by emergencies. This chapter emphasizes the often-overlooked aspect of physical fitness as a linchpin for thriving in adverse conditions. Understanding how to be comfortable with discomfort becomes a cornerstone for survival, giving individuals a crucial advantage over adversaries.

Comfortable with Discomfort: Mastering Environmental Challenges

Surviving in different weather conditions – be it rain, sleet, or snow – demands the ability to be comfortable with being uncomfortable. This skill is a key survival asset that must be cultivated independently. Operating in extreme temperatures or adverse weather conditions requires mental resilience and physical adaptability.

The Advantage of Adaptation

Being accustomed to discomfort provides a significant advantage in survival scenarios. If one is used to enduring physical challenges, such as being cold or physically fatigued, they possess a unique edge over those unaccustomed to such conditions. Adaptation becomes a secret weapon, enhancing one's ability to thrive in the face of adversity.

Initiative in Personal Fitness

Survival isn't solely about talk; it's about action. Many who discuss survival plans often neglect their own physical fitness. The ability to protect oneself, run from threats, and make split-second decisions hinges on personal fitness. Initiating a commitment to physical well-being is a proactive step towards bolstering the chances of survival.

The Unfit Survival Paradox

In the realm of survival enthusiasts, a paradox often emerges –
individuals who discuss survival plans may not necessarily be
physically fit themselves. The disconnection between talk and action
can jeopardize real preparedness. Being fit and healthy is not just
about looking the part; it's about having the physical capability to
endure and protect.

Choose to Run or Fight: The Physically Fit Advantage

In the face of threats, the physically fit have the flexibility to choose
when to run and when to stand their ground. Both scenarios require
peak physical condition. Fitness becomes a determining factor
between life and death, allowing individuals to navigate the
complexities of survival with agility and confidence.

Invest in Yourself: The Ultimate Survival Asset

In the pursuit of survival preparedness, investing in oneself is
paramount. Physical fitness is an investment that pays dividends in
emergencies. Building endurance, strength, and agility equips
individuals with the tools needed to navigate challenging situations,
protecting both themselves and their loved ones.

Start Now: Thriving Against All Odds

The call to action is clear – start now. Thriving against all odds
demands not only the acquisition of survival skills but also a
commitment to physical fitness. The synergy between mental
resilience and physical adaptability creates a survival framework that
can withstand the toughest challenges.

In conclusion, the physical requirements of survival extend far
beyond mere endurance. Being comfortable with discomfort,
adapting to environmental challenges, and maintaining peak physical
fitness are indispensable elements. Survival is not a passive

endeavor; it is an active commitment to personal well-being. Thriving in emergencies requires a holistic approach that incorporates both mental preparedness and physical fortitude.

Chapter 9: The Silent Prepper - Balancing Preparedness and Normalcy

In the world of survival, the wise prepper recognizes the importance of maintaining a low profile. This final chapter delves into the crucial aspect of discretion, urging individuals to stop boasting about their preparedness. The true prepper, like a shadow, remains hidden in plain sight, ensuring the security of their emergency action plan and loved ones.

The Pitfall of Over-Sharing

Discussing the intricacies of your preparedness openly can be a perilous move. Broadcasting the details of your plans, resources, and training not only compromises your security but also exposes those involved in your emergency action plan to potential risks. In a world where information is power, silence becomes a shield.

The Art of Incognito Preparedness

A genuine prepper embraces the art of incognito preparedness. Rather than becoming consumed by discussions of survival, the focus shifts to action. True preparedness lies in practicing your plan, not vocalizing it. Stealth becomes a key component of your survival strategy, ensuring that you remain off the radar of those unprepared.

Striking a Balance: Living and Preparing

The essence of a fulfilling life lies in striking a delicate balance between preparedness and normalcy. Constantly dwelling on potential emergencies can overshadow the beauty of everyday life. It is crucial to teach your family survival skills without turning every moment into a lesson. Life's joys and experiences should not be overshadowed by an obsessive focus on survival.

The Dangers of an All-Consuming Mindset

Some preppers become so consumed by their preparations that it eclipses the joy of living. Children, especially, should not grow up in an environment dominated by a doomsday mindset. It's essential to create a healthy balance, introducing survival concepts as part of enjoyable activities rather than a constant reminder of impending doom.

Teaching Survival through Everyday Adventures

Transforming survival lessons into engaging experiences can be achieved through creative approaches. Instead of discussing emergency water purification, make it a weekend science experiment. Explore the marvels of nature, turning learning into a family adventure. In doing so, survival becomes a part of life rather than an overwhelming presence.

Enjoying Life: The Ultimate Goal

Ultimately, the aim of preparedness is not just survival but thriving. A life well-lived encompasses moments of joy, growth, and shared experiences with loved ones. Constantly dwelling on an uncertain future detracts from the present. A true prepper knows how to balance preparedness with the simple joys that life offers.

The Silent Strength of the Wise Prepper

In conclusion, the wisdom of a prepper lies not in loud proclamations but in silent actions. The silent prepper finds strength in discretion, practicing preparedness without broadcasting it. By striking a balance between preparedness and normalcy, one can savor the richness of life while ensuring the safety and security of those they cherish.

Chapter 10: The Essential Arsenal – What You Need to Navigate Emergencies

In the face of uncertainty, your preparedness arsenal is the linchpin to survival. This chapter delves into the fundamental survival preps necessary to navigate myriad emergencies and sustain yourself and your loved ones.

1. Staples for Sustenance:
   - Dry goods like rice, salt, sugar, flour, and baking powder are versatile and can form the foundation of nourishing meals during extended emergencies.

2. Multifaceted Essentials:
   - Vinegar and cooking oil are invaluable. From basic nutrition to antibacterial properties, these items are indispensable. Honey, with its taste and antibacterial qualities, enhances your survival kit.

3. Emergency Food Stores:
   - Invest in survival food designed to endure up to 25 years when sealed and stored correctly. These provisions can be vital during prolonged emergencies.

4. Potable Water Strategy:
   - High-volume potable water storage, coupled with the ability to maintain it over time, is a game-changer. Master the art of water storage and purification devices to ensure a continuous water supply.

5. Respiratory Protection:
   - Acquire rated respiratory masks with cartridges tailored to anticipated threats. In a crisis, the ability to breathe can be the decisive factor in survival.

6. Air Filtration for Safe Spaces:

- Fortify your home against airborne contaminants with heavy-duty HEPA filters, duct tape, and plastic. Box fans aid in circulating air and maintaining a secure environment.

7. Emergency Medical Supplies:
  - A comprehensive medical kit, including trauma and respiratory items, is indispensable. Tourniquets, airway kits, and IV kits for major medical situations are crucial. Ensure you are well-versed in their usage.

8. Heating Solutions:
  - In the absence of power, a wood stove with external piping can provide warmth. Preparing for heating needs is paramount for survival.

9. Emergency Communications:
  - Handheld radios, walkie-talkies, citizens band radios, ham radios, and GRS are vital for staying connected. Effective communication is key during emergencies.

10. Clothing for All Seasons:
  - Adequate clothing for diverse conditions ensures you and your loved ones are prepared for any weather extremity.

11. Protection Essentials:
  - Items like firearms require not only acquisition but also meticulous cleaning and maintenance.

This comprehensive list forms the backbone of your survival strategy. Remember, each item is a necessity, and your preparedness ensures you are ready for whatever challenges arise. Assemble, prepare, and thrive in the face of uncertainty.

Chapter 11: Sustained Readiness through Vigilant Maintenance

In the symphony of preparedness, instruments need tuning to perfection. This chapter delves into the meticulous maintenance required to sustain the harmony of your survival plan, ensuring every piece of your preparedness ensemble is finely tuned and ready for the crescendo of any emergency.

1. Readiness Routine:
   - Establish a monthly readiness routine, a meticulous inspection to maintain your equipment. This proactive measure ensures everything is at its peak readiness for an immediate and effective response.

2. Fuel Stabilization:
   - Preserve the vitality of your fuel-powered assets through strategic fuel stabilization. Regular attention prevents breakdowns, guaranteeing your generators and vehicles are consistently ready. Fuel stability is a non-negotiable aspect of your preparedness plan.

3. Vehicle Maintenance:
   - Treat your vehicle as a reliable ally. Regularly check fluid levels, tire conditions, and engine components. In the world of preparedness, a well-maintained vehicle is a lifeline to safety.

4. Electronic Device Care:
   - Communication devices are the heartbeat of coordination. Regular checks, charging batteries to full capacity, and ensuring their good condition are paramount. In the realm of preparedness, reliable communication can be a deciding factor.

5. Water: Sustainment Planning:
   - For those relying on electrically-driven wells, meticulous sustainment planning is key. Regular scrutiny of stored water, frequent rotation, and the addition of necessary chemicals for prolonged storage ensure a consistent and pure water supply.

6. Dry Stores and Water Rotation:
  - Integrate a strategy for changing out dry stores after a specific period. Ensure a plan for using and replacing dry stores with fresh supplies, preventing spoilage over time. The same principle applies to water storage, where regular cycling and maintenance chemicals are essential during nonemergency times.

7. Symphony of Survival:
  - Dedicate a specific day each month to the symphony of survival. This is not just an inspection—it's an active engagement. Ensure every piece of equipment is in prime condition, ready for immediate deployment.

This chapter underscores the necessity of meticulous maintenance for sustained readiness. Your preparedness plan should be a dynamic composition, regularly fine-tuned to ensure peak performance when facing the unpredictable crescendo of an emergency.

Chapter 12: Active or Passive Survival

In a world simmering with discontent, where emotions run high, and a growing portion of the population is disgruntled with the state of affairs, survival is not only about physical prowess but a strategic dance of the mind. As the nation teeters on the edge, it's crucial to grasp the delicate balance between active and passive survival strategies.

Prolonged exposure to combat operations, a grim reality known by those who have been in the midst of chaos, inevitably leads to injury or worse. The art of survival often demands not confrontation, but strategic evasion. Learning to outsmart adversity, creating situations that tactically allow one to avoid conflict, becomes paramount. Those who have tasted the bitter realities of combat understand that avoiding a fight can be the key to living another day.

Amidst a society on edge, fueled by anger and discontent, the potential for confrontations escalates rapidly. In such times, it's imperative not to be swept away by the maelstrom. It's about ensuring you are not taken out in the prelude when you are meant to endure the main event.

Reviewing every option meticulously before engaging, understanding the delicate balance of risk versus reward, becomes the linchpin for the safety and survival of oneself and loved ones. Survival in an emergency is not a display of ego or bravado—it's about safeguarding family, a duty that transcends personal pride.

Remembering a fundamental principle of combat—always give your enemy an avenue to escape—highlights the importance of providing an exit strategy. Initiating conflict without an escape route for the adversary might lead to a more ferocious struggle as they fight desperately for survival.

In the theater of emergency situations, ego takes a back seat. It's not about bravado but about pragmatic decision-making. A prepared mind is a formidable weapon, and sometimes the smartest approach is to live to fight another day. Creating angles between oneself and danger, using strategic positioning, and understanding the terrain are all elements of mastering the battleground.

In cases of civil unrest or unprecedented national emergencies, threats often come to you. Owning every sector of your secure location, holding your ground, and making adversaries come to you can be a powerful defensive strategy. The high ground is a metaphorical and literal advantage, emphasizing the need to own and control the battleground.

In conclusion, active or passive survival is a nuanced dance between confrontation and strategic evasion. This chapter delves into the mindset required to navigate these complexities, emphasizing that in the face of danger, the ability to outthink and outmaneuver can often be a superior strategy than outright confrontation.

Navigating Chaos: A Practical Handbook for Modern Survival

Congratulations on completing "Navigating Chaos" – your essential guide to practical and modern survival. You've gained invaluable insights into building a resilient mindset, developing crucial skills, and crafting a comprehensive emergency action plan.

Take Action, Save Lives:
Now, armed with the knowledge within these pages, it's time to translate theory into practice. Share this wisdom with friends and family, empowering them to navigate the chaos of unexpected situations.

Share Your Story:
We invite you to share your personal experiences and how the strategies outlined in this book have impacted your life. Email us at markquartb@gmail.com with your stories – your journey might inspire others on their path to preparedness.

Thank you for choosing "Navigating Chaos." Your journey to preparedness has just begun.

Stay vigilant, stay prepared, and thrive in any scenario life throws your way.

Made in the USA
Las Vegas, NV
14 March 2024

87218364R00022